MW01517170

MULTIPLICATION
WORKBOOK MATH ESSENTIALS

Children's Arithmetic Books

PRODIGYWIZARD
BOOKS

Multiplication Exercises

Find the product.

Set 1

1.) $\begin{array}{r} 11 \\ \times\ 5 \\ \hline \end{array}$
2.) $\begin{array}{r} 3 \\ \times\ 4 \\ \hline \end{array}$
3.) $\begin{array}{r} 3 \\ \times\ 1 \\ \hline \end{array}$

4.) $\begin{array}{r} 7 \\ \times\ 0 \\ \hline \end{array}$
5.) $\begin{array}{r} 6 \\ \times\ 9 \\ \hline \end{array}$
6.) $\begin{array}{r} 9 \\ \times\ 8 \\ \hline \end{array}$

7.)   11
  x 6

8.)   3
  x 7

9.)   10
  x 5

10.)   9
  x 11

11.)   1
  x 0

12.) 10
  x 10

13.)
```
    5
x   4
_____
```

14.)
```
   12
x   1
_____
```

15.)
```
    2
x   3
_____
```

16.)
```
    1
x   1
_____
```

17.)
```
    2
x   5
_____
```

18.)
```
    3
x   7
_____
```

19.)   7
x 7
_____

20.)   1
x 11
_____

21.)   3
x 11
_____

22.)   6
x 8
_____

23.)   3
x 5
_____

24.)   6
x 6
_____

Set 2

1.)
$$\begin{array}{r} 5 \\ \times\ 2 \\ \hline \end{array}$$

2.)
$$\begin{array}{r} 9 \\ \times\ 3 \\ \hline \end{array}$$

3.)
$$\begin{array}{r} 5 \\ \times\ 0 \\ \hline \end{array}$$

4.)
$$\begin{array}{r} 11 \\ \times\ 1 \\ \hline \end{array}$$

5.)
$$\begin{array}{r} 9 \\ \times\ 10 \\ \hline \end{array}$$

6.)
$$\begin{array}{r} 5 \\ \times\ 8 \\ \hline \end{array}$$

7.)
```
   10
x   8
_____
```

8.)
```
    5
x  10
_____
```

9.)
```
   12
x  11
_____
```

10.)
```
   11
x   7
_____
```

11.)
```
    1
x  10
_____
```

12.)
```
    5
x   6
_____
```

13.)   3
      x 0
    ——————

14.)   1
      x 11
    ——————

15.)   11
      x 2
    ——————

16.)   11
      x 11
    ——————

17.)   9
      x 4
    ——————

18.)   2
      x 2
    ——————

19.)
$$\begin{array}{r} 8 \\ \times\ 3 \\ \hline \end{array}$$

20.)
$$\begin{array}{r} 5 \\ \times\ 4 \\ \hline \end{array}$$

21.)
$$\begin{array}{r} 9 \\ \times\ 2 \\ \hline \end{array}$$

22.)
$$\begin{array}{r} 11 \\ \times\ 10 \\ \hline \end{array}$$

23.)
$$\begin{array}{r} 2 \\ \times\ 7 \\ \hline \end{array}$$

24.)
$$\begin{array}{r} 1 \\ \times\ 8 \\ \hline \end{array}$$

Set 3

1.) 602
x   80
_____

2.) 321
x   30
_____

3.) 751
x   60
_____

4.) 960
x   10
_____

5.) 421
x   10
_____

6.) 774
x   20
_____

7.)   602
x   80
_____

8.)   321
x   30
_____

9.)   751
x   60
_____

10.)   960
x   10
_____

11.)   421
x   10
_____

12.)   774
x   20
_____

13.)   213
x   40
———————

14.)   329
x   60
———————

15.)   957
x   80
———————

16.)   605
x   40
———————

17.)   444
x   70
———————

18.)   416
x   70
———————

19.) 465
x   10
_____

20.) 184
x   60
_____

21.) 874
x   60
_____

22.) 260
x   90
_____

23.) 743
x   60
_____

24.) 453
x   10
_____

Set 4

1.) 16
x 40
_____

2.) 45
x 86
_____

3.) 31
x 23
_____

4.) 94
x 67
_____

5.) 40
x 26
_____

6.) 25
x 56
_____

7.) 16
   x 40
   ___

8.) 45
   x 86
   ___

9.) 31
   x 23
   ___

10.) 94
    x 67
    ___

11.) 40
    x 26
    ___

12.) 25
    x 56
    ___

13.) 86
x 72
___

14.) 30
x 38
___

15.) 94
x 40
___

16.) 76
x 80
___

17.) 55
x 87
___

18.) 68
x 17
___

19.) $\begin{array}{r} 67 \\ \times \ \ 74 \\ \hline \end{array}$

20.) $\begin{array}{r} 62 \\ \times \ \ 90 \\ \hline \end{array}$

21.) $\begin{array}{r} 874 \\ \times \ \ \ \ 60 \\ \hline \end{array}$

22.) $\begin{array}{r} 39 \\ \times \ \ 96 \\ \hline \end{array}$

23.) $\begin{array}{r} 88 \\ \times \ \ 27 \\ \hline \end{array}$

24.) $\begin{array}{r} 453 \\ \times \ \ \ \ 10 \\ \hline \end{array}$

Set 5

1.)   66
x   16

2.)   92
x   95

3.)   61
x   33

4.)   85
x   40

5.)   36
x   38

6.)   81
x   26

7.) 66
 x   16
 _____

8.) 92
 x   95
 _____

9.) 61
 x   33
 _____

10.) 85
 x   40
 _____

11.) 36
 x   38
 _____

12.) 81
 x   26
 _____

13.)   15
x   18
——————

14.)   72
x   84
——————

15.)   63
x   93
——————

16.)   17
x   74
——————

17.)   11
x   69
——————

18.)   67
x   73
——————

19.)   24
x   78
_____

20.)   28
x   19
_____

21.)   40
x   25
_____

22.)   38
x   32
_____

23.)   71
x   95
_____

24.)   83
x   21
_____

Set 6

1.)
$$\begin{array}{r} 802 \\ \times\ \ 90 \\ \hline \end{array}$$

2.)
$$\begin{array}{r} 480 \\ \times\ \ 30 \\ \hline \end{array}$$

3.)
$$\begin{array}{r} 104 \\ \times\ \ 60 \\ \hline \end{array}$$

4.)
$$\begin{array}{r} 586 \\ \times\ \ 50 \\ \hline \end{array}$$

5.)
$$\begin{array}{r} 756 \\ \times\ \ 60 \\ \hline \end{array}$$

6.)
$$\begin{array}{r} 963 \\ \times\ \ 70 \\ \hline \end{array}$$

7.)   802
x   90
_____

8.)   480
x   30
_____

9.)   104
x   60
_____

10.)   586
x   50
_____

11.)   756
x   60
_____

12.)   963
x   70
_____

13.)   359
x   10
_____

14.)   946
x   60
_____

15.)   838
x   80
_____

16.)   838
x   50
_____

17.)   882
x   50
_____

18.)   377
x   90
_____

19.) 380
x   70
_____

20.) 919
x   50
_____

21.) 874
x   60
_____

22.) 220
x   40
_____

23.) 516
x   50
_____

24.) 453
x   10
_____

Set 7

1.) 681
   x 70
   ‾‾‾‾‾‾

2.) 157
   x 60
   ‾‾‾‾‾‾

3.) 305
   x 20
   ‾‾‾‾‾‾

4.) 321
   x 30
   ‾‾‾‾‾‾

5.) 763
   x 60
   ‾‾‾‾‾‾

6.) 160
   x 60
   ‾‾‾‾‾‾

7.)   681
x   70

8.)   157
x   60

9.)   305
x   20

10.)   321
x   30

11.)   763
x   60

12.)   160
x   60

13.) 327
x   10
_____

14.) 558
x   60
_____

15.) 168
x   10
_____

16.) 406
x   10
_____

17.) 581
x   40
_____

18.) 753
x   40
_____

19.) 911
x   10
_____

20.) 586
x   70
_____

21.) 460
x   80
_____

22.) 744
x   70
_____

23.) 702
x   50
_____

24.) 599
x   20
_____

Set 8

1.) 2139
x   20
————————

2.) 2081
x   30
————————

3.) 1567
x   20
————————

4.) 1024
x   10
————————

5.) 1381
x   90
————————

6.) 1035
x   40
————————

7.) 2139
  x   20
  _____

8.) 2081
  x   30
  _____

9.) 1567
  x   20
  _____

10.) 1024
  x   10
  _____

11.) 1381
  x   90
  _____

12.) 1035
  x   40
  _____

13.) 1208
x   80
_____

14.) 1967
x   50
_____

15.) 2166
x   30
_____

16.) 1056
x   80
_____

17.) 1729
x   10
_____

18.) 2094
x   50
_____

19.)   1084
x   10
_____

20.) 1624
x   80
_____

21.) 2454
x   90
_____

22.)   2497
x   30
_____

23.) 1292
x   30
_____

24.) 1659
x   10
_____

Answers

Set 1

1.) $\begin{array}{r} 11 \\ \times\ 5 \\ \hline 55 \end{array}$
2.) $\begin{array}{r} 3 \\ \times\ 4 \\ \hline 12 \end{array}$
3.) $\begin{array}{r} 3 \\ \times\ 1 \\ \hline 3 \end{array}$
7.) $\begin{array}{r} 11 \\ \times\ 6 \\ \hline 66 \end{array}$
8.) $\begin{array}{r} 3 \\ \times\ 7 \\ \hline 21 \end{array}$
9.) $\begin{array}{r} 10 \\ \times\ 5 \\ \hline 50 \end{array}$

4.) $\begin{array}{r} 7 \\ \times\ 0 \\ \hline 0 \end{array}$
5.) $\begin{array}{r} 6 \\ \times\ 9 \\ \hline 54 \end{array}$
6.) $\begin{array}{r} 9 \\ \times\ 8 \\ \hline 72 \end{array}$
10.) $\begin{array}{r} 9 \\ \times 11 \\ \hline 99 \end{array}$
11.) $\begin{array}{r} 1 \\ \times\ 0 \\ \hline 0 \end{array}$
12.) $\begin{array}{r} 10 \\ \times 10 \\ \hline 100 \end{array}$

13.) $\begin{array}{r} 5 \\ \times\ 4 \\ \hline 20 \end{array}$
14.) $\begin{array}{r} 12 \\ \times\ 1 \\ \hline 12 \end{array}$
15.) $\begin{array}{r} 2 \\ \times\ 3 \\ \hline 6 \end{array}$
19.) $\begin{array}{r} 7 \\ \times\ 7 \\ \hline 49 \end{array}$
20.) $\begin{array}{r} 1 \\ \times 11 \\ \hline 11 \end{array}$
21.) $\begin{array}{r} 3 \\ \times 11 \\ \hline 33 \end{array}$

16.) $\begin{array}{r} 1 \\ \times\ 1 \\ \hline 1 \end{array}$
17.) $\begin{array}{r} 2 \\ \times\ 5 \\ \hline 10 \end{array}$
18.) $\begin{array}{r} 3 \\ \times\ 7 \\ \hline 21 \end{array}$
22.) $\begin{array}{r} 6 \\ \times\ 8 \\ \hline 48 \end{array}$
23.) $\begin{array}{r} 3 \\ \times\ 5 \\ \hline 15 \end{array}$
24.) $\begin{array}{r} 6 \\ \times\ 6 \\ \hline 36 \end{array}$

Set 2

1.) $\begin{array}{r} 5 \\ \times\ 2 \\ \hline 10 \end{array}$
2.) $\begin{array}{r} 9 \\ \times\ 3 \\ \hline 27 \end{array}$
3.) $\begin{array}{r} 5 \\ \times\ 0 \\ \hline 0 \end{array}$
7.) $\begin{array}{r} 10 \\ \times\ 8 \\ \hline 80 \end{array}$
8.) $\begin{array}{r} 5 \\ \times 10 \\ \hline 50 \end{array}$
9.) $\begin{array}{r} 12 \\ \times 11 \\ \hline 132 \end{array}$

4.) $\begin{array}{r} 11 \\ \times\ 1 \\ \hline 11 \end{array}$
5.) $\begin{array}{r} 9 \\ \times 10 \\ \hline 90 \end{array}$
6.) $\begin{array}{r} 5 \\ \times\ 8 \\ \hline 40 \end{array}$
10.) $\begin{array}{r} 11 \\ \times\ 7 \\ \hline 77 \end{array}$
11.) $\begin{array}{r} 1 \\ \times 10 \\ \hline 10 \end{array}$
12.) $\begin{array}{r} 5 \\ \times\ 6 \\ \hline 30 \end{array}$

13.) $\begin{array}{r} 3 \\ \times\ 0 \\ \hline 0 \end{array}$
14.) $\begin{array}{r} 1 \\ \times 11 \\ \hline 11 \end{array}$
15.) $\begin{array}{r} 11 \\ \times\ 2 \\ \hline 22 \end{array}$
19.) $\begin{array}{r} 8 \\ \times\ 3 \\ \hline 24 \end{array}$
20.) $\begin{array}{r} 5 \\ \times\ 4 \\ \hline 20 \end{array}$
21.) $\begin{array}{r} 9 \\ \times\ 2 \\ \hline 18 \end{array}$

16.) $\begin{array}{r} 11 \\ \times 11 \\ \hline 121 \end{array}$
17.) $\begin{array}{r} 9 \\ \times\ 4 \\ \hline 36 \end{array}$
18.) $\begin{array}{r} 2 \\ \times\ 2 \\ \hline 4 \end{array}$
22.) $\begin{array}{r} 11 \\ \times 10 \\ \hline 110 \end{array}$
23.) $\begin{array}{r} 2 \\ \times\ 7 \\ \hline 14 \end{array}$
24.) $\begin{array}{r} 1 \\ \times\ 8 \\ \hline 8 \end{array}$

Set 3

1.) 602 x 80 48160	2.) 321 x 30 9630	3.) 751 x 60 45060	7.) 602 x 80 48160	8.) 321 x 30 9630	9.) 751 x 60 45060
4.) 960 x 10 9600	5.) 421 x 10 4210	6.) 774 x 20 15480	10.) 960 x 10 9600	11.) 421 x 10 4210	12.) 774 x 20 15480
13.) 213 x 40 8520	14.) 329 x 60 19740	15.) 957 x 80 76560	19.) 465 x 10 4650	20.) 184 x 60 11040	874 x 60 52440
16.) 605 x 40 24200	17.) 444 x 70 31080	18.) 416 x 70 29120	22.) 260 x 90 23400	23.) 743 x 60 44580	24.) 453 x 10 4530

Set 4

1.) 16 x 40 640	2.) 45 x 86 3870	3.) 31 x 23 713	7.) 16 x 40 640	8.) 45 x 86 3870	9.) 31 x 23 713
4.) 94 x 67 6298	5.) 40 x 26 1040	6.) 25 x 56 1400	10.) 94 x 67 6298	11.) 40 x 26 1040	12.) 25 x 56 1400
13.) 86 x 72 6192	14.) 30 x 38 1140	15.) 94 x 40 3760	19.) 67 x 74 4958	20.) 62 x 90 5580	43 x 64 2752
16.) 76 x 80 6080	17.) 55 x 87 4785	18.) 68 x 17 1156	22.) 39 x 96 3744	23.) 88 x 27 2376	24.) 453 x 10 4530

Set 5

1.) 66
x 16
———
1056

2.) 92
x 95
———
8740

3.) 61
x 33
———
2013

7.) 66
x 16
———
1056

8.) 92
x 95
———
8740

9.) 61
x 33
———
2013

4.) 85
x 40
———
3400

5.) 36
x 38
———
1368

6.) 81
x 26
———
2106

10.) 85
x 40
———
3400

11.) 36
x 38
———
1368

12.) 81
x 26
———
2106

13.) 15
x 18
———
270

14.) 72
x 84
———
6048

15.) 63
x 93
———
5859

19.) 24
x 78
———
1872

20.) 28
x 19
———
532

21.) 40
x 25
———
1000

16.) 17
x 74
———
1258

17.) 11
x 69
———
759

18.) 67
x 73
———
4891

22.) 38
x 32
———
1216

23.) 71
x 95
———
6745

24.) 83
x 21
———
1743

Set 6

1.) 802
x 90
———
72180

2.) 480
x 30
———
14400

3.) 104
x 60
———
6240

7.) 802
x 90
———
72180

8.) 480
x 30
———
14400

9.) 104
x 60
———
6240

4.) 586
x 50
———
29300

5.) 756
x 60
———
45360

6.) 963
x 70
———
67410

10.) 586
x 50
———
29300

11.) 756
x 60
———
45360

12.) 963
x 70
———
67410

13.) 359
x 10
———
3590

14.) 946
x 60
———
56760

15.) 838
x 80
———
67040

19.) 380
x 70
———
26600

20.) 919
x 50
———
45950

21.) 604
x 50
———
30200

16.) 838
x 50
———
41900

17.) 882
x 50
———
44100

18.) 377
x 90
———
33930

22.) 220
x 40
———
8800

23.) 516
x 50
———
25800

24.) 599
x 20
———

Set 7

1.) 681 x 70 47670	2.) 157 x 60 9420	3.) 305 x 20 6100	7.) 681 x 70 47670	8.) 157 x 60 9420	9.) 305 x 20 6100
4.) 321 x 30 9630	5.) 763 x 60 45780	6.) 160 x 60 9600	10.) 321 x 30 9630	11.) 763 x 60 45780	12.) 160 x 60 9600
13.) 327 x 10 3270	14.) 558 x 60 33480	15.) 168 x 10 1680	19.) 911 x 10 9110	20.) 586 x 70 41020	460 x 80 36800
16.) 406 x 10 4060	17.) 581 x 40 23240	18.) 753 x 40 30120	22.) 744 x 70 52080	23.) 702 x 50 35100	24.) 599 x 20 11980

Set 8

1.) 2139 x 20 42780	2.) 2081 x 30 62430	3.) 1567 x 20 31340	7.) 2139 x 20 42780	8.) 2081 x 30 62430	9.) 1567 x 20 31340
4.) 1024 x 10 10240	5.) 1381 x 90 124290	6.) 1035 x 40 41400	10.) 1024 x 10 10240	11.) 1381 x 90 124290	12.) 1035 x 40 41400
13.) 1208 x 80 96640	14.) 1967 x 50 98350	15.) 2166 x 30 64980	19.) 1084 x 10 10840	20.) 624 x 80 129920	21.) 2454 x 90 220860
16.) 1056 x 80 84480	17.) 1729 x 10 17290	18.) 2094 x 50 104700	22.) 2497 x 30 74910	23.) 1292 x 30 38760	24.) 1659 x 10 16590

CPSIA information can be obtained
at www.ICGtesting.com
Printed in the USA
LVHW060917230420
654317LV00011B/1318

9 781683 232681